A Journey Through Holy Week

A Journey Through Holy Week

From the Gospel of Matthew

JUSTIN MILLER

RESOURCE *Publications* · Eugene, Oregon

A JOURNEY THROUGH HOLY WEEK
From the Gospel of Matthew

Resource Publications
An Imprint of Wipf and Stock Publishers
199 W. 8th Ave., Suite 3
Eugene, OR 97401

www.wipfandstock.com

PAPERBACK ISBN: 978-1-5326-6872-2
HARDCOVER ISBN: 978-1-5326-6874-6
EBOOK ISBN: 978-1-5326-6880-7

Manufactured in the U.S.A.   JANUARY 31, 2019

To my children Kaleb, Ella, Isaac, and Eden. My constant petition in prayer is that you would savor the Savior who infinitely saves and satisfies all who believe.

Contents

Acknowledgements

By God's grace I'm blessed with a wife, who adores Jesus, children God has gifted us with to nurture in the Lord, and a church family who deeply desires to know Him and make Him known. This project was possible because of God's grace in those influences. Thank you Tonna and Eric, who gave thought to the need for a Holy Week exposition and picked out the hymns for each day. Thank you, Pastor Buddy and Pastor Allen, for taking time reading through the book for clarity of content. I'm honored to serve alongside you brothers. Thank you to Brandon, Lori, and Melissa for reading and editing this work. Thank you to my beloved mother for your help with editing. For my church family, I'm immensely blessed by the privilege of being your pastor and am grateful for your encouragement. The greatest "thank you" goes to my wife, JoDawn. You are my beautiful best friend. I thank God for you and rise up to call you blessed in our Lord Jesus. For "many women have done excellently, but you surpass them all."

Introduction

GOD'S PEOPLE IN THE Old Testament found themselves in messes because they failed to consistently reflect on God's revealed character and past redemptive works. The book of Judges begins with God's people forgetting God's great acts of deliverance and straying into all sorts of idolatry (Judges 1–2). Unfortunately, this was the constant pattern in the history of God's people during the Old Testament. Is it any wonder that the Law of God outlined three festivals a year to be attended by all Jewish males to reflect on God's grace and Word? In Deuteronomy 6:9–12, the people were instructed to inscribe God's Word on their doorposts, as a constant reminder of God's character and commands. In the Gospels, Jesus instituted two ordinances for the church to consistently reflect on His sacrifice to save sinners. Throughout Scripture God calls His forgetful people to remember His past work so they may see His everlasting glory. This study examines the events of Holy Week from the Gospel of Matthew as a way to reflect on and remember what our Lord Jesus accomplished on behalf of sinners. Holy Week begins the first Sunday before Easter and reflects on the events of Jesus' last days leading into His crucifixion and resurrection. A journey through Holy Week, in the Gospel of Matthew, brings us afresh to the last days of Jesus culminating in His death and resurrection. My prayer for each person who takes this journey is their affections are stirred for the King of kings who laid down His life for His people.

I

Palm Sunday

Matthew 21:1–11

1Now when they drew near to Jerusalem and came to Bethphage, to the Mount of Olives, then Jesus sent two disciples, 2 saying to them, "Go into the village in front of you, and immediately you will find a donkey tied, and a colt with her. Untie them and bring them to me. 3 If anyone says anything to you, you shall say, 'The Lord needs them,' and he will send them at once." 4 This took place to fulfill what was spoken by the prophet, saying,

> "Say to the daughter of Zion,
> 'Behold, your king is coming to you,
> humble, and mounted on a donkey,
> on a colt, the foal of a beast of burden.'"

6 The disciples went and did as Jesus had directed them. 7 They brought the donkey and the colt and put on them their cloaks, and he sat on them. 8 Most of the crowd spread their cloaks on the road, and others cut branches from the trees and spread them on the road. 9 And the crowds that went before him and that followed him were shouting, "Hosanna to the Son

of David! Blessed is he who comes in the name of the Lord! Hosanna in the highest!" 10 And when he entered Jerusalem, the whole city was stirred up, saying, "Who is this?" 11 And the crowds said, "This is the prophet Jesus, from Nazareth of Galilee." [1]

I HAVE AN ANNOUNCEMENT!

"I HAVE AN ANNOUNCEMENT!" Those words are usually accompanied by a stunning revelation that is either a cause for celebration, or for great concern. Jesus announced publicly, His identity as the Messianic King on Palm Sunday. It was His public "I have an announcement; I'm the Messiah!" The apostle Matthew, who penned this Gospel account, comments on Jesus fulfilling Scripture for the announcement of the arrival of the Messiah (Zechariah 9:9, which Matthew outlines in verses 4–5) through His riding into Jerusalem on a colt. Matthew is the only Gospel to mention two animals (the donkey and the colt).[2] The Jews, during this time, understood Zechariah 9:9 as a reference to the Messiah who would ride into Jerusalem peaceably on a donkey's colt.[3] Jesus, with great intentionality, has His disciples retrieve the donkey and colt so that He may announce He is the Messiah.

The crowds, per verse 8, were there spreading their cloaks and palm branches on the road. Jesus, in what must have been a breath-taking moment, calmly rode into Jerusalem on the colt of a donkey. The crowds erupted with praise proclaiming per verse 9, "Hosanna to the Son of David! Blessed is he who comes in the name of the Lord! Hosanna in the Highest!" These words of praise came from Psalm 118:25–26 and the word "Hosanna" is a transliteration from the Hebrew word meaning "Save!" which was a word of praise and petition.[4] They called Jesus the "Son of David"

---

1. *The Holy Bible: English Standard Version.* (2016). (Mt 21:1–11). Wheaton, IL: Crossway Bibles.

2. Barker, Gospel of Matthew, 93–94.

3. Barker, Gospel of Matthew, 93.

4. Barker, Gospel of Matthew, 94.

which stressed His identity as the long-awaited Messiah who from David's seed would assume the throne and rule over God's people. They called out, "Blessed is the One who comes in the name of the Lord." Jesus is from God the Father, and the people were praising God for the Messiah who had come.

The whole city was stirred up with the possibility of the Lord Jesus being the long-awaited Messiah who had finally come to save His people. What caused such a stir? Why had the people come to this conclusion? Shortly before Jesus rode into Jerusalem on a donkey, the apostle John tells us the Lord Jesus had raised Lazarus from the dead (John 11:1–44). Per the apostle John (John 11:45-John 12:11), this event brought many of the Jews to the expectation that Jesus was the Messiah they were waiting for. The people were speculating with the following reasoning: "Who but God's anointed could raise the dead to life? This must be the Messiah." As news of this miracle spread in Jerusalem, in light of the coming Passover celebration, many of the Jews searched for this Jesus who had the power to raise the dead to life! During Passover, Messianic expectations were high because of what the Jews were celebrating. They were celebrating God's deliverance of them from the bondage of slavery in Egypt, through His judgments against Egypt, culminating in the death of the first born throughout Egypt. The angel of death had passed over the people of Israel's homes because they had heeded God's command to put the blood of a Lamb over their door posts and homes. The people were reflecting on God's past deliverance from bondage and the news spread of a man who raised the dead to life. A man who was from the line of David. The expectation of a deliverer to free the people from Rome, rose afresh in the hearts of all those in Jerusalem. As Jesus rode into Jerusalem announcing publicly that He was the Messiah, the people's hearts were stirred and ablaze with Messianic fervor and expectancy. However, Jesus would not be the Messiah they expected. He first came to save God's people from their sin, not the rule of Rome. Jesus announced on Palm Sunday that He is the Messiah. This Palm Sunday let us remember that our King rode into Jerusalem on a donkey's colt. His identity could not be any clearer. He is the

Messiah who, as the angel told Joseph before Jesus' birth, "will save his people from their sins."[5]

THE KING HAS COME TO CLAIM HIS KINGDOM

The Messiah has come! He is the King who laid down His life for His people and took His life up again. It would be amiss to not mention the reality that this triumphant entry into Jerusalem fore-shadowed a second coming. The phrase, "He who comes in the name of the Lord," (Matthew 21:9) Jesus quoted in reference to His second coming in Matthew 23:39 as He lamented over Jerusalem. Jesus, the Messiah, came first to save sinners as the suffering servant. He is coming again as the conquering king. The Messiah has come and is coming again! Palm Sunday celebrates that the Messiah came to save sinners and reminds us of His future return.

DISCUSSION QUESTIONS

1. Why did Jesus ride into Jerusalem on a donkey on Palm Sunday?

2. What caused the crowds to gather with palm branches proclaiming Jesus as the Messiah?

3. How did the Jews misunderstand Jesus as Messiah?

4. What does Jesus as Messiah mean Biblically and how should that affect us today?

---

5. *The Holy Bible: English Standard Version.* (2016). (Mt 1:21). Wheaton, IL: Crossway Bibles.

HYMN FOR PALM SUNDAY—
"ALL HAIL THE POWER OF JESUS' NAME"

All hail the pow'r of Jesus' Name!
Let angels prostrate fall
Bring forth the royal diadem,
And crown Him Lord of all!
Ye chosen seed of Israel's race,
Ye ransomed from the fall,
Hail Him Who saves you by His grace,
And crown Him Lord of all!
Let every kindred, every tribe,
On this terrestrial ball,
To Him all majesty ascribe,
And crown Him Lord of all!
Oh, that with yonder sacred throng
We at His feet may fall!
We'll join the everlasting song,
And crown Him Lord of all!

2

Monday Blues

Matthew 21:12–17

12 And Jesus entered the temple and drove out all who sold and bought in the temple, and he overturned the tables of the money-changers and the seats of those who sold pigeons. 13 He said to them, "It is written, 'My house shall be called a house of prayer,' but you make it a den of robbers."

14 And the blind and the lame came to him in the temple, and he healed them. 15 But when the chief priests and the scribes saw the wonderful things that he did, and the children crying out in the temple, "Hosanna to the Son of David!" they were indignant, 16 and they said to him, "Do you hear what these are saying?" And Jesus said to them, "Yes; have you never read,

"'Out of the mouth of infants and nursing babies
you have prepared praise?'"

17 And leaving them, he went out of the city to Bethany and lodged there.[1]

---

1. *The Holy Bible: English Standard Version.* (2016). (Mt 21:12–17). Wheaton, IL: Crossway Bibles.

MONDAY BLUES

MANY OF US WILL at times get the Monday blues. The weekend is over and it is back to work. Back to the daily grind for another week. Jesus, after the emotionally-gripping Palm Sunday, starts His Monday in a powerful way. He curses the fig tree because it had no figs and by day's end it withered. It is symbolic of God's Son coming to Israel to find it fruitless in its worship and leaving it cursed in its rejection of the Messiah. He goes into the temple and cleanses it from the unacceptable and abominable practices that were taking place before God! He then, while in the courts of the temple, heals the blind and lame to the praises of "Hosanna Son of David!"

Now Matthew's Gospel account seems to imply in verse 12 that Jesus entered the temple immediately after His triumphal entry on Palm Sunday. However, the other Gospel accounts convey that Jesus returned to Bethany and on Monday entered the temple to cleanse it (Mark 11:11–17, Luke 19:45–46).[2] Jesus enters into the temple courts (the center of the worship of God in Israel) and cleanses it with righteous, controlled indignation. This was actually the second time Jesus did this in the temple courts. The first was at the onset of His public ministry as recorded by the apostle John in John 2:13–22.[3]

Why the Temple Cleansing?

The temple had become a place where God's people were being taken advantage of monetarily as the chief priests had established a system that profited them personally.[4] Temple money was the only currency accepted for pilgrims to use in order to purchase animals in temple grounds. Animals that were "ironically enough," pre-approved by the priests. There was a fee for the money transfer from Greek and Roman currency into temple currency. The

2. Barbieri, Gospel of Matthew, 68.

3. Barker, Gospel of Matthew, 95.

4. MacArthur, The Jesus Answer Book, 140–141.

animals were sold at very inflated prices to the profit of the merchants and priests. The temple where God's people were to worship had become a market. One commentator put it the following way: "As Messiah, Jesus entered the temple area. His indignation was directed toward those who had changed the character of the temple from a place of prayer into a place of corrupt commercialism. Many were making their living from the temple and the sacrifices purchased there. They insisted that in the temple the people could not use money that had been circulating in society, but had to change their money into temple money first, for a fee, and then use the temple money to purchase animals for sacrifice, at inflated prices. Such extortion was completely contrary to the temple's purposes."[5] Imagine the scene. What was to be holy and sacred was a marketplace filled with animals, manure, and commercialism. Where the glory of God was to be on display, the greed of man was being exalted. Is it any wonder our Lord raged against such things? For the temple was where God's manifest presence was to dwell with man.

Jesus' Response

Jesus' response to such perversion of the worship of God was planned. In Mark 11:11 the Lord Jesus had observed the temple court's proceedings after His triumphal entry on Palm Sunday, and He went back that night to Bethany. Monday morning, the Lord Jesus marched right into the temple after having cursed the fig tree for its lack of figs, symbolizing God's judgment on Israel, and intentionally overturned the money changer tables and drove out the livestock and the pigeons. He pronounced judgment in verse 13 when He stated, "It is written, 'My house shall be called a house of prayer,' but you make it a den of robbers."[6] Jesus' response was judgment. But it was judgment followed by great mercy!

5. Barbieri, Gospel of Matthew, pg. 68.
6. *The Holy Bible: English Standard Version.* (2016). (Mt 21:13). Wheaton, IL: Crossway Bibles.

The Result

After Jesus cast the merchants and money changers out, He manifested God's glory in the temple as He healed those in need (the blind and lepers, per verse 14). The crowds praised Him in verse 15 for His display of God's glory in healing the hurting; all while the chief priests and scholars chided him in anger for his actions against the merchants and money changers. Jesus performed the same actions, but it garnished different responses. The leaders of Israel rejected and hated the praise Jesus was receiving. The people adored Him for what He had done in the temple to cleanse it and to bring healing to those who were blind and lame. Today, Jesus brings such diverse reactions when He is presented from Holy Scripture. Some respond with reception most with rejection.

The Tale of Two Men

There is a story Jesus taught in Luke 18:9–14, where two men approached God in the temple area. One man was a tax collector, a traitor to his nation. He collected money on behalf of his own people's oppressors. He obtained wealth from the struggling laborers of Israel. He was a corrupt, selfish, and greedy man. The other was a religious man, devoted in his obedience to the Law. He tithed to God from his earnings, and was determined to keep every tradition of his people. Both men went into the court of the temple to approach God's presence. The religious man of the strictest part of the people's region (a Pharisee) boasted before God of his works. He compared himself to the unworthy tax collector, who he saw from the corner of his eye in the same area. He left there that day satisfied in his religion, yet doomed to face an eternity of judgment before God. The tax collector would not even look up towards God's heavenly throne. He felt the weight of his sin and his guilt. He had nothing to offer God. All his life he had lived for self and pursued his own pleasures. Broken over his life and sinful heart, he squeaked out, "Have mercy on me, a sinner!" Jesus said in this story the tax collector went home forgiven forever and saved before God. The same truth was available to both the Pharisee and tax collector. Why did one receive forgiveness and the other judgment? The reality is one knew he needed a Savior, and the other approached God through a religion of his own making, like Cain before him in Genesis 4, only to find rejection.

REMEMBERING MONDAY OF HOLY WEEK

On this Monday around 2000 years ago, Jesus gave life to those who were blind and lame, yet was rejected by those whose lives were consumed with a religion of their own making that offended God. May we approach God this Monday as beggars needing the bread of life. May we come to God asking Him to cleanse our hearts as His Son cleansed the temple!

DISCUSSION QUESTIONS

1. What was the state of the temple and the worship of God therein?

2. Why did Jesus cleanse the temple?

3. What about Israel's religion offended God?

4. How are we to approach God?

HYMN FOR MONDAY—
"HOW GREAT THOU ART"

1. O Lord my God, when I in awesome wonder
Consider all the worlds Thy hands have made
I see the stars, I hear the rolling thunder
Thy power throughout the universe displayed

[Refrain]

Then sings my soul, my Savior God, to Thee
How great Thou art, how great Thou art
Then sings my soul, my Savior God, to Thee
How great Thou art, how great Thou art!

2. When through the woods, and forest glades I wander
And hear the birds sing sweetly in the trees
When I look down, from lofty mountain grandeur
And see the brook, and feel the gentle breeze

3. And when I think, that God, His Son not sparing
Sent Him to die, I scarce can take it in
That on the Cross, my burden gladly bearing
He bled and died to take away my sin

4. When Christ shall come, with shout of acclamation
And take me home, what joy shall fill my heart
Then I shall bow, in humble adoration
And then proclaim: "My God, how great Thou art!"

3

Tuesday Troubles

Matthew 21:23; 24:1–2; 26:1–2

23 And when he entered the temple, the chief priests and the elders of the people came up to him as he was teaching, and said, "By what authority are you doing these things, and who gave you this authority?"[1]

1Jesus left the temple and was going away, when his disciples came to point out to him the buildings of the temple. 2 But he answered them, "You see all these, do you not? Truly, I say to you, there will not be left here one stone upon another that will not be thrown down." [2]

1When Jesus had finished all these sayings, he said to his disciples, 2 "You know that after two days the Passover is coming, and the Son of Man will be delivered up to be crucified."[3]

1. *The Holy Bible: English Standard Version.* (2016). (Mt 21:23). Wheaton, IL: Crossway Bibles.

2. *The Holy Bible: English Standard Version.* (2016). (Mt 24:1–2). Wheaton, IL: Crossway Bibles.

3. *The Holy Bible: English Standard Version.* (2016). (Mt 26:1–2). Wheaton, IL: Crossway Bibles.

TUESDAY TROUBLES

OUT OF THE FRYING pan and into the fire. We all know the reality of that phrase. From one moment of conflict to another. Jesus, on Monday, was in the frying pan of righteous indignation against the perversion of the worship of God in the temple. With a perfect and pure love for His Father, Jesus responded by cleansing the temple of the market and consumerism that had overtaken it. As He entered the temple courts on Tuesday, He found Himself in the fire of unsaved sinful man's response to the cleansing work of God. He stepped out of the frying pan of Monday into the fire of Tuesday. The fire of Tuesday centered around the rebukes and objections of the Jewish leaders, but finished with Jesus' loving instruction and care for His disciples as He prepared them for the time ahead when He would not be with them physically.

A SYNOPSIS OF TUESDAY
AND A REMINDER

Jesus begins His Tuesday in Matthew 21 with a firestorm of debate against the religious leaders. His actions on Monday produced a disdain and hatred for Him that would only be satisfied in His execution. His parables in response to their questioning of His authority further spurned their hatred of Him (Matthew 21:23–22:14). These religious leaders wanted Him gone, yet faced a problem. Jesus was incredibly popular with the crowds. The religious sects and their leaders came up with some questions to trap Him in Matthew 22:15–40. They picked questions surrounding the debates of Jesus' day. Every question He answered in such a way that they no longer could, or wanted to, ask Him anything further. He put them in their proverbial place through His various responses, and then asked a question which they could not answer. He followed that up with a stinging string of woes, thereby condemning the Jewish leader's hypocrisy. In pronouncing seven woes against the Scribes and Pharisees in Matthew 23, Jesus stood resolutely against their external system of works that was void of genuine faith and love in God the Father. He calls the Pharisees blind guides and white washed tombs. Many view Jesus as a revolutionary who was all love and yet nothing else. Those who view Jesus as such, probably have not come across Matthew 23 or Revelation 19–20.

During the rest of Tuesday, the Lord Jesus shifts His focus from confrontation to discipleship. He spends the rest of the day teaching His disciples in Matthew 24–25 about the coming days ahead of them, after His departure and the end that would come. He, after His teaching of His disciples, reminds them of His pending crucifixion in Matthew 26:1–2. Now, there is a lesson here for us found in Tuesday's troubles. Something to help us endure the unending uncertainty, and the consistent claims the world is coming to an end.

THE WORLD IS ENDING!!!

Have you ever noticed after natural disasters or cataclysmic events many people (sometimes religious people) began propagating the whole "the world is ending" narrative? They often describe a purer time and the current tribulation of the days they are in as a "sign" the end has come. On Tuesday of Holy Week in Matthew 24, Jesus reminds His disciples that disaster, war, and destruction wrought by mankind is par for the course in their coming days. We are not to be surprised by wars and the rumor of wars. Rather we are to heed our Lord's command to His disciples, possible only by His sovereign grace, that all who endure to the end will be saved (Matthew 24:13).

THE REMINDER OF TUESDAY

This Tuesday we are reminded the Lord Jesus resolutely proclaimed God's glory and stood against human effort to obtain salvation before God (The Pharisees' doctrine). He proclaimed woes on a system that taught you could only receive the grace of God through the works of the Law and tradition of the elders. He taught His disciples of the coming kingdom and its everlasting consummation. He reminded them that the shadow of the cross loomed. Today, let us reflect on Jesus entering the fire of confrontation from the frying pan of His work to cleanse the temple. We, as God's people, must engage in the daily fires of carrying our crosses as we follow Jesus, the one who cleansed us from all sin and made us the new temple of God the Holy Spirit (1 Corinthians 6:19). For by God's grace alone we endure to the end, knowing the days are dark and evil, yet the light of a day whose brightness will know no end has already begun to rise from the east.

DISCUSSION QUESTIONS

1. Why were the Jewish leaders angry with Jesus?

2. As Jesus left the temple on Tuesday His focus shifted to whom and what?

3. What was the last thing Jesus said to His disciples on Tuesday as recorded in Matthew?

4. What do we see concerning the intentions of the religious leaders at the end of Tuesday?

5. What was it about the Pharisees' and Scribes' doctrine that Jesus disdained? (Hint: it was all based around how one enters the kingdom of God)

HYMN FOR TUESDAY—
"IT IS WELL WITH MY SOUL"

1. When peace, like a river,
attendeth my way,
When sorrows like sea billows roll;
Whatever my lot,
Thou hast taught me to say,
"It is well, it is well with my soul
Chorus: It is well (it is well)
with my soul (with my soul)
It is well, it is well with my soul

2. Though Satan should buffet,
though trials should come,
Let this blessed assurance control,
That Christ has regarded
my helpless estate,
And hath shed His own blood for my soul.

3. My sin, oh the bliss
of this glorious thought!
My sin, not in part but the whole,
Is nailed to the cross,
and I bear it no more,
Praise the Lord, praise the Lord, O my soul!

4. And Lord haste the day
when the faith shall be sight,
The clouds be rolled back as a scroll;
The trump shall resound,
and the Lord shall descend,
Even so, it is well with my soul.

4

Wednesday Preparation

Matthew 26:6–16

6 Now when Jesus was at Bethany in the house of Simon the leper, 7 a woman came up to him with an alabaster flask of very expensive ointment, and she poured it on his head as he reclined at table. 8 And when the disciples saw it, they were indignant, saying, "Why this waste? 9 For this could have been sold for a large sum and given to the poor." 10 But Jesus, aware of this, said to them, "Why do you trouble the woman? For she has done a beautiful thing to me. 11 For you always have the poor with you, but you will not always have me. 12 In pouring this ointment on my body, she has done it to prepare me for burial. 13 Truly, I say to you, wherever this gospel is proclaimed in the whole world, what she has done will also be told in memory of her."

14 Then one of the twelve, whose name was Judas Iscariot, went to the chief priests 15 and said, "What will you give me if I deliver him over to you?" And they paid him thirty pieces of silver. 16 And from that moment he sought an opportunity to betray him. [1]

1. *The Holy Bible: English Standard Version.* (2016). (Mt 26:6–16). Wheaton, IL: Crossway Bibles.

WEDNESDAY'S PREPARATION FOR BURIAL AND BETRAYAL

Every funeral is a reminder that we as human beings will face death. In 1 Corinthians 15:22 we are told "all in Adam die." Every one of us inherits Adam's sinful nature and guilt (Romans 5:12–17). Yet, Jesus' death was different. He was sinless. He voluntarily, for the glory of His Father, laid His life down in our stead. Wednesday was a day of burial preparation and betrayal. On Wednesday, Jesus is at the house of Simon the Leper attending a meal in His honor after having previously raised Lazarus from the dead in the same town. There was a woman in attendance in Matthew 26:7 (identified as Mary the sister of Lazarus and Martha in John 12:3) who breaks open a flask of expensive alabaster ointment and pours it on his head. The apostle John, in his Gospel, suggests it is worth a working man's salary for the year. This ointment was possibly from the nard plant native to India.[2]

The disciples, with Judas as the spokesperson here per John 12:4–5, were in disagreement, and even somewhat appalled at Jesus. Jesus proclaimed, in verse 12, that the expensive anointment was to prepare Him for burial. This act of reverence, per Jesus in verse 13, would be upheld in honor wherever the Gospel was proclaimed. Judas leaves the scene in verse 14 to betray Jesus. He goes to the chief priests and agrees to deliver Jesus for 30 pieces of silver. Verse 16 tells us that Judas, from that point on, looked for an opportunity to betray Jesus.

WHY DID JUDAS BETRAY JESUS?

Judas betraying Jesus came after Jesus pointedly confronted Judas' objection to the expensive ointment being used to anoint Jesus, instead of being sold to help the poor. Judas' real motives behind his objection are conveyed in John 12:4–6. He was not interested in helping the poor, but rather he was interested in profiting off of Jesus' ministry. Judas, the only non-Galilean, was the treasurer and

2. Barker, Gospel of Matthew, 117.

stole from the funds given to Jesus and his disciples. He was upset the ointment was used for Jesus instead of sold and the money given to the treasury, which Judas was in charge of.

Judas was greedy and selfish. His god was his desire for gain. He must have seen Jesus as a means to an end; a political Messiah who would elevate him to glory untold. At least that is what he appears to have thought. However, Jesus' insistent declarations that He was going to die on a cross, and in light of the rebuke, must have been a blow to Judas' pride. Judas chose to betray Jesus. Bible students have pondered the question, "Why?" What was the core motivation for Judas to betray Jesus? What was his motive?

Two Possible Motives????

1. He was disillusioned by Jesus' failure to establish a political kingdom, and his hopes for material gain seemed doomed.
2. His love for money moved him to salvage something for himself. Ultimately, he was the tool of a defeated devil (cf. Luke 22:3; John 13:2, 27).[3]

Judas' disappointment and disillusionment betrayed Jesus. His love for money propelled him to the purse of the priests, possibly with the thought that he could salvage something from this situation. Judas outwardly professed Jesus for perceived benefits Jesus would give. His life was a tragedy, and his betrayal was an abomination for all time. However, let us never forget that Jesus sovereignly ruled over His betrayal. He knew whom He had chosen and what Judas would do (John 6:70–71). God ordained the choice of Judas to bring Jesus to the cross to bear the justice of God for His church (Acts 4:27–28). God ruled over Judas' evil intent and actions for the good of God's people for all time to the endless glory of the eternal Triune God.

3. Grassmick, Gospel of Mark. 175.

PREPARED FOR BURIAL AND BETRAYED

Our Lord was prepared for burial and betrayed on Wednesday. Praise God for our Savior who was tempted in all ways as we are yet without sin. Praise God we have a High Priest who knows the sting of betrayal. We all have a Judas, and maybe some of us have been one. Regardless, Wednesday reminds us that God the Son added humanity and truly experienced it all to save sinners such as us.

DISCUSSION QUESTIONS

1. What was the significance of Mary pouring the ointment on Jesus' head?

2. Why was Judas upset?

3. Judas made what arrangement with the chief priests?

4. Why did Judas betray Jesus?

5. How is Jesus facing death and betrayal an encouragement to us?

HYMN FOR WEDNESDAY—
"GRACE GREATER THAN OUR SIN"

Marvelous grace of our loving Lord,
Grace that exceeds our sin and our guilt.
Yonder on Calvary's mount outpoured,
there where the blood of the Lamb was spilt.

Refrain:
Grace, grace God's grace,
Grace that will pardon and cleanse within;
Grace, grace God's grace,
Grace that is greater than all our sin.

Dark is the stain that we cannot hide,
what can avail to take it away?
Look! There is flowing a crimson tide;
Whiter than snow you may be today.

Marvelous, infinite matchless grace,
freely bestowed on all who believe;
All who are longing to see His face,
will you this moment His grace receive?

5

Thursday Supper

Matthew 26:26–39, 47–50

26 Now as they were eating, Jesus took bread, and after blessing it broke it and gave it to the disciples, and said, "Take, eat; this is my body." 27 And he took a cup, and when he had given thanks he gave it to them, saying, "Drink of it, all of you, 28 for this is my blood of the covenant, which is poured out for many for the forgiveness of sins. 29 I tell you I will not drink again of this fruit of the vine until that day when I drink it new with you in my Father's kingdom." 30 And when they had sung a hymn, they went out to the Mount of Olives. 31 Then Jesus said to them, "You will all fall away because of me this night. For it is written, 'I will strike the shepherd, and the sheep of the flock will be scattered.' 32 But after I am raised up, I will go before you to Galilee." 33 Peter answered him, "Though they all fall away because of you, I will never fall away." 34 Jesus said to him, "Truly, I tell you, this very night, before the rooster crows, you will deny me three times." 35 Peter said to him, "Even if I must die with you, I will not deny you!" And all the disciples said the same.

36 Then Jesus went with them to a place called Gethsemane, and he said to his disciples, "Sit here, while

I go over there and pray." 37 And taking with him Peter and the two sons of Zebedee, he began to be sorrowful and troubled. 38 Then he said to them, "My soul is very sorrowful, even to death; remain here, and watch with me." 39 And going a little farther he fell on his face and prayed, saying, "My Father, if it be possible, let this cup pass from me; nevertheless, not as I will, but as you will."

47 While he was still speaking, Judas came, one of the twelve, and with him a great crowd with swords and clubs, from the chief priests and the elders of the people. 48 Now the betrayer had given them a sign, saying, "The one I will kiss is the man; seize him." 49 And he came up to Jesus at once and said, "Greetings, Rabbi!" And he kissed him. 50 Jesus said to him, "Friend, do what you came to do." Then they came up and laid hands on Jesus and seized him.[1]

THE PROFOUND AND POWERFUL EVENTS OF A SUPPER ON THURSDAY

HAVE YOU EVER HAD a day you just knew would stay with you forever? Maybe it was your wedding day, or perhaps the day you lost a loved one. We all have those type of days, which no matter how much time passes, the events that took place on that day can still be easily recalled to our minds. They are days, whose events, have shaped and influenced who we are today. Thursday was one of those days for Peter and the other disciples. It was also a day that set a precedent for Christ's church for every generation henceforth. It was a day where Jesus commanded them to remember what took place. A supper on Thursday that would be repeated by God's people for all time. It was a significant day for the disciples and for all Christians for all time.

---

1. *The Holy Bible: English Standard Version.* (2016). (Mt 26:17–75). Wheaton, IL: Crossway Bibles.

THE PASSOVER MEAL

In Matthew 26:17–19 the disciples are sent to prepare the Passover meal. The Passover was celebrated every year by the Jews. It was instituted on the day of days for Moses and the generation of Hebrews who witnessed God's wonders in His deliverance of them from cruel bondage and abject slavery. God chose to perform this deliverance through Moses and Aaron, whereby God brought nine plagues upon Egypt that culminated in a tenth judgment. The tenth judgment God used to finally break Pharaoh's hard-hearted unwillingness to let the Hebrews go was the death of all the first born in Egypt. God struck down all the first born but "passed over" all the houses of the people of Israel that had the blood of a Lamb on its door posts and lentil. Pharaoh relinquished and let the people go after this judgment of God against Egypt. The people of Israel were commanded to commemorate this event every year by slaughtering one Passover lamb per household and eating unleavened bread with herbs.

The people in Jesus' time celebrated the Passover beginning in midafternoon of Thursday. The lambs, one per household, were brought to the temple court where the priests sacrificed them. The Lamb's fat was burned on the altar of burnt offering and the blood put at the foot of the altar. After sunset, the household (a group of about 10 people), would gather to eat the Passover, which would have been roasted with bitter herbs.[2] The head of the household would give thanks for the Passover and wine.[3] A preliminary course of greens and bitter herbs was served, followed by the Passover. There were four different servings of wine.[4]

Jesus chose the celebration of God's wrath passing over the people of Israel to institute the Lord's Supper. Why? Think about the connection between the two. For all time, the Lord's Supper would be a reminder to God's people in the church age that God's wrath passed over us because of the shed blood and body given of

2. Barker, Gospel of Matthew, 119.

3. Barker, Gospel of Matthew, 119.

4. Barker, Gospel of Matthew, 119.

the perfect Lamb of God on the cross of Calvary. For all time, it would be the new memorial of God's greatest act of deliverance, where He made rebels into forever family through shed blood of Christ Jesus.

THE LORD'S SUPPER

In what must have been a moment for the disciples that would stand still in time, Jesus took the unleavened bread in Matthew 26:26, commanding the disciples to take it, for it represented His body given on the cross. In verse 27–28, he took the cup of wine, declaring the wine represented His blood shed for the remission of the sins of many. He told them this was the memorial of His sacrifice which brings the New Covenant between God and man, whereby a person's sins are forgiven and the wrath of God passes over them if they repent and apprehend Christ's work on the cross through faith alone, by grace alone. Jesus then follows up this memorial with the reality that as they (the disciples) and we (the church) partake in this, we remember also that Christ Jesus is coming again, whereby we will sit with him to celebrate at the wedding feast of the Lamb (verse 29). Jesus, on Thursday, instituted one of two ordinances that His church was forever to partake in.

Why does this matter to us? Jesus commands His disciples, and thereby us, to take the Lord's Supper to reflect on and remember His sacrifice (body given, blood shed) for the forgiveness of the sins of His church. We are a forgetful people. Jesus institutes the Lord's Supper so that we may stop all we are doing and reflect on what He has done for us for all time to the glory of God the Father. Think about who we are. We are sinners, rebels, and transgressors. Think about who God is. He is holy, pure, perfect, and radiantly majestic. How can holy God and sinful man dwell together? We are infinitely apart, but the work of Jesus bridges the gap and brings sinful people, purified by the blood of the Lamb (Revelation 7:14), into the presence of God forever!

Thursday is the day of preparation for the Passover and the institution of the Lord's Supper, but it is also the agony of

Gethsemane as our Lord Jesus faced the pending cross and the coming wrath of God for sinners.

GARDEN OF GETHSEMANE

After Jesus institutes the Lord's Supper, He and His disciples leave for the garden of Gethsemane singing a hymn. Upon entrance into the garden Jesus brings the inner three (Peter, James, and John) with Him to keep watch as He prays in the garden while the other disciples are at a further distance. Overcome with agony at the coming wrath of God, Jesus cries out in prayer, as His disciples sleep. "My Father let this cup pass from me, but not my will but thy will be done." (verse 39). What is the cup Jesus is referring to?

The cup refers to the coming wrath of God that Jesus would soon drink in full, down to the last drop. The imagery of a cup was commonly used in the Old Testament of God's wrath (Psalms 75:7–8; Isaiah 51:19, 22; Jeremiah 25:15–16; etc.).[5] Jesus did not fear the Jewish leadership and their mockery, nor did He fear the Roman governor and his legions. He did not fear the pain of suffering or the taste of death. Jesus feared the wrath of God. God the Son knew better than anyone what the wrath of God was, and He in His deity was going to experience it for all God's beloved chosen from eternity past. Jesus would experience infinite wrath on the cross, and the thought of such an event brought agony moments before His betrayal. His disciples slept at their Lord's moment of need as He in His perfection resolved fully to endure the wrath of God for sinners to the glory of the Father.

Judas enters the garden in verse 47, apparently familiar with that as a meeting place for Jesus and His disciples, and betrays Jesus. Peter will later deny Jesus three times and Jesus will endure a mockery of Jewish trials. But for now, this Thursday, let us focus on the meaning of the Lord's Supper and the garden of Gethsemane. God the Son added humanity ultimately to be the propitiation (wrath bearer) for His people. Thursday reminds of us of the

---

5. Barker, *Gospel of Matthew*, 122.

meaning of Friday's cross. Jesus, in our place, took our penalty. He endured God's everlasting wrath for God's eternally loved people. This is what Thursday is about.

DISCUSSION QUESTIONS

1. What is the Passover?

2. What is the significance of the Lord Jesus instituting the Lord's Supper on the Passover?

3. Why is the Lord's Supper the greater Passover Celebration?

4. What is the cup Jesus referred to in the Garden of Gethsemane?

5. What does the Thursday of Holy Week communicate to us concerning the work of Jesus for sinners?

HYMN FOR THURSDAY—"I STAND AMAZED IN THE PRESENCE"

I stand amazed in the presence of Jesus the Nazarene
And wonder how He could love me, a sinner condemned unclean.

Refrain:
How marvelous, how wonderful
And my song shall ever be!
How marvelous, how wonderful
Is my Savior's love for me!

For me it was in the garden, He prayed not my will but Thine,
He had no tears for His own griefs but sweat drops of blood for mine.

He took my sins and my sorrows, He made them His very own,
He bore the burden to Calvary, and suffered and died alone.

6

"Good" Friday

Matthew 27:35–37, 45–54, 57–61

35 And when they had crucified him, they divided his garments among them by casting lots. 36 Then they sat down and kept watch over him there. 37 And over his head they put the charge against him, which read, "This is Jesus, the King of the Jews."

45 Now from the sixth hour there was darkness over all the land until the ninth hour. 46 And about the ninth hour Jesus cried out with a loud voice, saying, "Eli, Eli, lema sabachthani?" that is, "My God, my God, why have you forsaken me?" 47 And some of the bystanders, hearing it, said, "This man is calling Elijah." 48 And one of them at once ran and took a sponge, filled it with sour wine, and put it on a reed and gave it to him to drink. 49 But the others said, "Wait, let us see whether Elijah

will come to save him." 50 And Jesus cried out again with a loud voice and yielded up his spirit.

51 And behold, the curtain of the temple was torn in two, from top to bottom. And the earth shook, and the rocks were split. 52 The tombs also were opened. And many bodies of the saints who had fallen asleep were raised, 53 and coming out of the tombs after his resurrection they went into the holy city and appeared to many. 54 When the centurion and those who were with him, keeping watch over Jesus, saw the earthquake and what took place, they were filled with awe and said, "Truly this was the Son of God!" [1]

57 When it was evening, there came a rich man from Arimathea, named Joseph, who also was a disciple of Jesus. 58 He went to Pilate and asked for the body of Jesus. Then Pilate ordered it to be given to him. 59 And Joseph took the body and wrapped it in a clean linen shroud 60 and laid it in his own new tomb, which he had cut in the rock. And he rolled a great stone to the entrance of the tomb and went away. 61 Mary Magdalene and the other Mary were there, sitting opposite the tomb.[2]

THE CLIMAX OF HISTORY

JESUS' CROSS IS THE climax of human history. It is the peak moment by which God glorifies Himself the greatest and rectifies the fall of man. It is the moment of glory and redemption. It is the fulfillment of the Old Testament Covenant and the giving of the New Testament Covenant. All of human history revolves around the Son of God and His cross. The goodness of "Good Friday" is the work of Jesus on the cross; not the injustice of man, but the goodness of God to reconcile sinners to Himself through the death of Jesus on the cross. The author of Hebrews puts it this way, "2 looking to Jesus, the founder and perfecter of our faith, who for the joy

1. *The Holy Bible: English Standard Version.* (2016). (Mt 27:32–54). Wheaton, IL: Crossway Bibles.

2. *The Holy Bible: English Standard Version.* (2016). (Mt 27:57–61). Wheaton, IL: Crossway Bibles.

that was set before him endured the cross, despising the shame, and is seated at the right hand of the throne of God."[3] Jesus looked past the shame, as He hung on the cross, to God's glory in redeeming a people for Himself that would find their joy in Him forever.

OVERVIEW OF EVENTS LEADING TO CROSS

Thursday night, Jesus was betrayed by Judas in Gethsemane. He was brought before Annas and Caiaphas and tried. No testimony brought before Jesus agreed. Yet, He was declared worthy of death because of the charge of blasphemy brought against Him by the council (the Sanhedrin). That morning the Sanhedrin met and officially pronounced the judgment and shipped Jesus to Pilate where He was tried, sent to Herod, sent back to Pilate, scourged and condemned (*Matthew 27:1–61, Mark 15:1–47, Luke 23:1–56, John 18:28–19:42*). This Good Friday we are reflecting on the result of the unjust trials of Jesus that God sovereignly used. We are going to reflect on the climax of history. The cross of Jesus, whereby He endured the righteous punishment of God in the place of sinners so that we may have His reward of life everlasting, is the meaning of Good Friday and the peak of history!

JESUS' CRUCIFIXION

Jesus was crucified per Matthew 27:35. What is fascinating, is Matthew does not expound upon all the details of what it meant to be crucified. Matthew did not need to elaborate. Everyone in the first century Roman world knew very well what crucifixion entailed. It was a common method of carrying out the death sentence in the Roman world, and was reserved only for non-Roman citizens and the worst criminals.[4] It was a slow process and could last for days.

---

3. *The Holy Bible: English Standard Version.* (2016). (Heb 12:1–2). Wheaton, IL: Crossway Bibles.

4. Martin, Gospel of Luke, 262..

The cause of death for crucifixion could come from asphyxiation, as the victim bound or nailed to the cross would have to lift themselves up on the wood via their dislocated arms to garnish air for their lungs.[5] Other causes of death were heart failure, dehydration, and hypovolemic shock. [6] Regardless, it was a painful and excruciating way to die. It was meant to deter rebellion against Rome. Jesus per verse 35 was crucified between two criminals. He was mocked by the religious leaders, and endured hours on the cross.

THE REAL PAIN OF THE CROSS

While the physical pain was substantial, the endurance of God's infinite punishment for every one of His people's sins was the true terror to the soul of our Lord Jesus. 2 Corinthians 5:21 states, "21 For our sake he made him to be sin who knew no sin, so that in him we might become the righteousness of God."[7] God the Father placed all of the rebellion and guilt of His people upon Jesus and then punished Jesus with His infinite everlasting judgment, as the world went dark while Jesus hung on a cross. This was the cup of wrath Jesus dreaded in the garden. In verse 47 of Matthew 27 Jesus called out to God the Father, "My God, My God why have you forsaken me?" He quoted Psalms 22:1 as He suffered in agony feeling the wrath of God and forsaking of God's love. In essence Jesus endured the frown of God so we may forever have God's smile over us. As He declared in victory "It is finished!" (John 19:30) He gave up His Spirit and died in Matthew 27:50. He did not whimper out, but with a loud voice He declared, "It is finished!" and gave up His Spirit. The next verse (Matthew 27:51–54) shows the effects of His sacrifice. The curtain between the Holy Place and the Most Holy Place (where God's manifest presence was thought to dwell reigning over His people) in the temple was torn in two from the top down. Jesus' sacrifice now brings all God's people

5. Fiensy, Crucifixion. *The Lexham Bible Dictionary*.

6. Fiensy, Crucifixion. *The Lexham Bible Dictionary*.

7. *The Holy Bible: English Standard Version*. (2016). (2 Co 5:21). Wheaton, IL: Crossway Bibles.

into God's manifest presence. No longer is access to the most Holy God barred. It is forever opened to all redeemed by Jesus. Many of the dead believers of God were raised (Jesus crucifixion was the means by which God did this), the earth shook violently, and a Roman Centurion (experienced with death) looked in awe at the man on the cross declaring Him to be God. He was declared dead, and His side pierced with the result of water and blood flowing out. His legs unbroken, His body given, and His blood shed for the remission of the sins of many.

The rest of Friday sees Jesus in Matthew 27:57–61 buried in Joseph of Arimathea's tomb by Joseph and Nicodemus. The climax of history has taken place! The Son of God paid the sin debt of a rebellious, wicked people to the glory of God the Father forever on Good Friday! The response that "Good" Friday calls forth in the world is to repent and believe (Acts 2:38, Acts 16:31). To be precise, for those who do not know God through faith alone in Jesus alone, the call is to turn from sin (rebellion against God as our Creator) to faith in the perfect Son of God who died the death we deserve so we may have the reward that He earned in His righteousness. For those who know God through faith alone in Jesus alone, the response is to keep looking to Jesus and walk in the works that He prepared for His people beforehand to walk in, which is all God's grace (Ephesians 2:8–10).

DISCUSSION QUESTIONS

1. Describe the events that lead to the cross?

2. What did Jesus endure in His physical suffering?

3. What did Jesus accomplish on behalf of God's people?

4. What makes Friday of Holy Week "Good Friday?"

5. What should your response be to "Good" Friday?

HYMN FOR GOOD FRIDAY—
"JESUS PAID IT ALL"

I hear the Savior say, "Thy strength indeed is small,
Child of weakness watch and pray, find in me Thine all in all."
Jesus paid it all, all to Him I owe,
Sin had left a crimson stain, He washed it white as snow.
Lord, now indeed I find, Thy power and Thine alone
Can change the leper's spots and melt a heart of stone.
For nothing good have I where by Thy grace to claim;
I'll wash my garments white in the blood of Calvary's lamb.
And when, before the throne I stand in Him complete;
"Jesus died my soul to save," my lips shall still repeat.
Jesus paid it all, all to Him I owe,
Sin had left a crimson stain, He washed it white as snow.

7

Forgotten Saturday

Matthew 27:62–66

62 The next day, that is, after the day of Preparation, the chief priests and the Pharisees gathered before Pilate 63 and said, "Sir, we remember how that impostor said, while he was still alive, 'After three days I will rise.' 64 Therefore order the tomb to be made secure until the third day, lest his disciples go and steal him away and tell the people, 'He has risen from the dead,' and the last fraud will be worse than the first." 65 Pilate said to them, "You have a guard of soldiers. Go, make it as secure as you can." 66 So they went and made the tomb secure by sealing the stone and setting a guard. [1]

FORGOTTEN

IT IS EASY, AS time progresses, to forget many of the details that occur in-between major events in our life. Most anyone can remember the day they were married or perhaps their first home. However, it is the in-between details that often are taken for

1. *The Holy Bible: English Standard Version.* (2016). (Mt 27:62–66). Wheaton, IL: Crossway Bibles.

granted and even lost. Saturday of Holy Week is often forgotten. It is a day between two gigantic events. Friday our Lord Jesus was crucified, and Sunday He rises from the dead. Those two events are not just significant for first century people, but for all people from all centuries. However, sandwiched between those two days is Saturday.

SATURDAY SETS THE STAGE FOR SUNDAY

The Jewish leaders remembering what Jesus taught concerning His resurrection, though they did not believe, in Matthew 27:62–66 go to Pilate to procure guards for Jesus' tomb and to place a Roman seal over it (verse 65–66). The Jewish leaders are afraid that the disciples, or others, will steal Jesus' body and then proclaim that He has risen from the dead. They are procuring against the event of fraud. The Roman guards seal the tomb with a cord across the stone and a wax seal which was the official Roman seal.[2] What is even more fascinating, is the Jewish leaders are breaking their own Sabbath Laws by going into Pilate in order to ensure Jesus of Nazareth stays in the tomb. Their commitment to the end of His influence is substantial and steady.[3] The guards provide the maximum security possible for the tomb. [4] There is no getting Jesus out of the tomb by human standards without extreme Roman reaction and judgment.

FALLING INTO A PIT

Proverbs 26:27 states, "27 Whoever digs a pit will fall into it, and a stone will come back on him who starts it rolling."[5] The plans people make to harm, or keep something from happening, some-

2. Barbieri, Gospel of Matthew, 92.

3. France, Gospel of Matthew. 944.

4. France, Gospel of Matthew, 944.

5. *The Holy Bible: English Standard Version.* (2016). (Pr 26:27). Wheaton, IL: Crossway Bibles.

times is the very thing that ultimately comes back to hurt and hinder them. That is the point of Proverbs 26:27. The writer pictures a person who digs a pit to capture and harm someone else as they walk along the road, yet they themselves fall into their own trap to their own destruction. We see a principle here that was evident in the life of Joseph in the Old Testament. His brothers sold him into slavery. They thought him to be gone from their sight forever. Eventually, they bowed before what seemed to be a powerful Egyptian governor, as they were in need of food to sustain their existence, only to learn it was Joseph. Joseph's brothers originally threw him into a pit only to find themselves in a pit of their own. However, Joseph lovingly forgave and cared for them. When his father died, the brothers sent to him for forgiveness. Joseph brings them before him and states: "Do not fear, for am I in the place of God. *As for you, you meant evil against me, but God meant it for good,* to bring it about that many people should be kept alive, as they are today. 21 So do not fear; I will provide for you and your little ones." Thus, he comforted them and spoke kindly to them.[6] Joseph's brothers meant their betrayal of him for his harm, but God sovereignly ordained their actions and used it for the good of Joseph's brothers and the world. God reigns over all, and even the actions of those in rebellion against Him serve His decreed purposes. With the events of Saturday, we see God's characteristics on display as all-knowing and all powerful. How, though?

Think about it. God sovereignly allows the Sanhedrin to plot with Pilot to make the tomb of Jesus secure. He has ordained to raise Jesus from the dead and show Him alive beyond a shadow of doubt. This act of deliberation by Pilate and the Jewish leaders will ultimately be one of the greatest indirect evidences for the resurrection of Jesus. For on Sunday, Jesus rose from the dead, the stone was moved away, and the Roman seal broken. However, the disciples, who were said to have stolen the body by the guards bribed by the Jewish leaders in Matthew 28:11–15, were never prosecuted by the Roman authorities, though they supposedly had broken the

---

6. *The Holy Bible: English Standard Version.* (2016). (Ge 50:19–21). Wheaton, IL: Crossway Bibles.

seal. This would have been an offense against Rome. The reality is the disciples did not steal the body or Rome would have arrested them for rebellion against the empire by breaking a Roman seal. Not only does Rome leave them alone, even the Jewish leaders in the book of Acts do not use the lie of the disciples stealing the body to try and refute the growing Gospel movement that bursts forth after Pentecost. Saturday's events are all about the leaders digging a pit that they themselves will fall into. God, in His sovereignty, is using this event, which the leaders intended for evil against the movement of Jesus, for the good of the Gospel going out into the world for all generations.

DISCUSSION QUESTIONS

1. What happened on Saturday?

2. How do we see God's sovereign hand using His enemies for His glory?

3. What did Jesus accomplish on behalf of God's people?

A HYMN FOR SATURDAY—
"WHEN I SURVEY THE WONDROUS CROSS"

When I survey the wondrous cross,
on which the prince of glory died,
My richest gain I count but loss
and pour contempt on all my pride.
Forbid it Lord that I should boast,
save in the death of Christ my God;
All the vain things that charm me most,
I sacrifice them to His blood.
See, from His head, His hands,
His feet, Sorrow and love flow mingled down.
Did e'er such love and sorrow meet,
or thorns compose so rich a crown?
Were the whole realm of nature mine,
that were a present far too small;
Love so amazing so divine,
demands my soul, my life, my all.

8

Resurrection Sunday

Matthew 28

28 Now after the Sabbath, toward the dawn of the first day of the week, Mary Magdalene and the other Mary went to see the tomb. 2 And behold, there was a great earthquake, for an angel of the Lord descended from heaven and came and rolled back the stone and sat on it. 3 His appearance was like lightning, and his clothing white as snow. 4 And for fear of him the guards trembled and became like dead men. 5 But the angel said to the women, "Do not be afraid, for I know that you seek Jesus who was crucified. 6 He is not here, for he has risen, as he said. Come, see the place where he lay. 7 Then go quickly and tell his disciples that he has risen from the dead, and behold, he is going before you to Galilee; there you will see him. See, I have told you." 8 So they departed quickly from the tomb with fear and great joy, and ran to tell his disciples. 9 And behold, Jesus met them and said, "Greetings!" And they came up and took hold of his feet and worshiped him. 10 Then Jesus said to them, "Do not be afraid; go and tell my brothers to go to Galilee, and there they will see me."

11 While they were going, behold, some of the guard went into the city and told the chief priests all that had taken place. 12 And when they had assembled with the elders and taken counsel, they gave a sufficient sum of money to the soldiers 13 and said, "Tell people, 'His disciples came by night and stole him away while we were asleep.' 14 And if this comes to the governor's ears, we will satisfy him and keep you out of trouble." 15 So they took the money and did as they were directed. And this story has been spread among the Jews to this day.

16 Now the eleven disciples went to Galilee, to the mountain to which Jesus had directed them. 17 And when they saw him, they worshiped him, but some doubted. 18 And Jesus came and said to them, "All authority in heaven and on earth has been given to me. 19 Go therefore and make disciples of all nations, baptizing them in the name of the Father and of the Son and of the Holy Spirit, 20 teaching them to observe all that I have commanded you. And behold, I am with you always, to the end of the age."[1]

THE RESURRECTION IS THE RECEIPT

PAUL THE APOSTLE STATED, "*17 And if Christ has not been raised, your faith is futile, and you are still in your sins.*"[2] The resurrection is the validation of the person and work of the Lord Jesus. If there is no resurrection, there is no Christian faith. It is the Great Receipt from the Father given to all those who believe in Jesus. The resurrection is the only way we can know we are truly forgiven and Jesus is genuinely God and man. Recently, I filled my car up with gas. I swiped the credit card in the machine to pay for the gas now in the tank of my car. How do I know the payment was taken in exchange for the gas that went into my tank? The receipt.

1. *The Holy Bible: English Standard Version.* (2016). (Mt 28:1–20). Wheaton, IL: Crossway Bibles.

2. *The Holy Bible: English Standard Version.* (2016). (1 Co 15:17). Wheaton, IL: Crossway Bibles.

The receipt verifies that money was given in exchange for the gas for my car to run. The resurrection is the receipt that our sin debt was paid by the cross of Jesus so that we may know God and dwell with Him forever. Paul says it this way, "Jesus our Lord, who was delivered up for our trespasses and raised for our justification." [3] Jesus was raised for our justification, meaning to validate the work of the cross on our behalf.

YOU CANNOT MAKE THIS STUFF UP

The apostle Matthew in Matthew 28:1–10 outlines the first person to see the resurrected and glorified Jesus. It was Mary Magdalene. The significance of this cannot be understated. It was not Peter or John who first saw Jesus risen. It was not James, the half-brother of Jesus. It was Mary. In a society where women were second class citizens, the prominence given here to a woman and women in the other Gospel accounts (Mark 16:1–8) is profoundly powerful.[4]

In a society in which women were second-class citizens, their prominence in the Gospel accounts, especially that of Jesus' resurrection, is striking. A woman's testimony in this culture would not have been considered valid. However, Matthew describes Mary's testimony of the resurrected Jesus (Matthew 28:1–10), and for all time, shows this is not a story a first century A.D. mind would have made up. You cannot make this stuff up! If the disciples had indeed invented the idea of Jesus' resurrection, after having stolen His body, which was the lie perpetuated by the Jewish leaders to protect their position (Matthew 28:11–15), they would never have chosen a woman as the first eye witness to Jesus' resurrection. It would not have been considered credible. Yet, Matthew describes the events as they occurred. Jesus rose from the dead and first appeared to Mary and the other woman per Mark 16:1–8. Jesus rose from the dead.

3. *The Holy Bible: English Standard Version.* (2016). (Ro 4:24–25). Wheaton, IL: Crossway Bibles.

4. France, Gospel of Matthew, 944.

THE RESURRECTION POINTS US FORWARD TO THE MISSION OF CHRIST

Matthew in Matthew 28:16–20 then conveys Jesus appearing to His disciples in Galilee before His ascension. We know from 1 Corinthians 15:5–11 that Jesus made appearances to all His disciples and even 500 people at one time, which for all time confirmed His resurrection with eye witness testimony, that could not be denied. Jesus, between His resurrection and ascension, was on the earth 40 days (Acts 1:3). Before He was taken to heaven, He tells His disciples, the foundation of the church, that all authority has been given to Him (Matthew 28:18). He then moves to command them to make disciples as they go in the world, baptizing those whom God saves, and teaching all that Jesus had commanded them (Matthew 28:19). He reminds them in verse 20 at the close of the Gospel of Matthew, that He will always be with them. The Resurrected Jesus was returning to the glory He shared with the Father (John 17:5). He commissions the foundation of the church (the apostles per Ephesians 2:20), thereby the church itself, to go into the world and make disciples. The resurrection is meant to move us to the mission of Christ. The reason? Jesus lives and reigns over the nations. Therefore, in and under His authority, we go to claim the reward of His sufferings.

AS WE GO

As we go in everyday life, we are sovereignly placed where we live to share the good news that Jesus has risen and all who repent of their sins and believe in the Lord Jesus will be saved (Romans 10:9). We have family members, friends, co-workers, neighbors, community members, associates, our nation, and all the nations before us. We are called to live in light of a resurrected King and Savior who commanded us to make Him known and call out His people from the world. Those who heed the call, we are to see baptized in the name of the Triune God who saved them and taught the commands of Christ in the local church. This is an impossible task, humanly speaking. Mankind's hearts are depraved and dead in their natural state. However, God has given His Spirit to empower His people to endure in the faith. He has given His people His Word to share knowing that God's decrees will not be thwarted, cannot be thwarted, and have never been thwarted! Also, let us never forget that it is by the work of God's Spirit through the proclamation of God's Word the spiritually dead come to life and the depravity of man is overcome (Ezekiel 37). Jesus will have the reward of His sufferings (Acts 20:28)! His resurrection assures us that the transaction has already occurred. The receipt was given. Therefore, we go into the world, confident of God's grace and power, with Gospel urgency for the Lamb who was slain has risen and will have His reward!

DISCUSSION QUESTIONS

1. **What happened on Sunday?**

2. **What does the Resurrection validate?**

3. **What is the significance of the first eye witnesses of Jesus being risen?**

4. **What was the response of the religious leaders?**

5. **What should be our response to the reality of the resurrected King per Matthew 28:16–20?**

HYMN FOR RESURRECTION SUNDAY— "CHRIST AROSE"

Low in the grave He lay—Jesus, my Savior
Waiting the coming day—Jesus, my Lord!

Refrain:
Up from the grave He arose,
with a mighty triumph for His foes
He arose a victor from the dark domain
And He lives forever with the saints to reign
He arose! He arose!
Hallelujah! Christ arose!

Vainly they watch His bed—Jesus, my Savior!
Vainly they seal the dead—Jesus, my Lord!

Death cannot keep His prey—Jesus, my Savior!
He rolled the stone away—Jesus, my Lord!

Bibliography

The Holy Bible: English Standard Version. (2016). Wheaton, IL: Crossway Bibles.

Barbieri, L. A., Jr. (1985). Matthew. In J. F. Walvoord & R. B. Zuck (Eds.), *The Bible Knowledge Commentary: An Exposition of the Scriptures* (Vol. 2). Wheaton, IL: Victor Books.

Barker, K. L. (1994). *Expositor's Bible Commentary (Abridged Edition: New Testament)*. Grand Rapids, MI: Zondervan Publishing House.

Fiensy, D. A. (2016). Crucifixion. In J. D. Barry, D. Bomar, D. R. Brown, R. Klippenstein, D. Mangum, C. Sinclair Wolcott, . . . W. Widder (Eds.), *The Lexham Bible Dictionary*. Bellingham, WA: Lexham Press.

France, R. T. (1994). Matthew. In D. A. Carson, R. T. France, J. A. Motyer, & G. J. Wenham (Eds.), *New Bible commentary: 21st century edition* (4th ed.). Leicester, England; Downers Grove, IL: Inter-Varsity Press.

Grassmick, J. D. (1985). Mark. In J. F. Walvoord & R. B. Zuck (Eds.), *The Bible Knowledge Commentary: An Exposition of the Scriptures* (Vol. 2). Wheaton, IL: Victor Books.

MacArthur, John. The Jesus Answer Book. Thomas Nelson. Nashville, TN. 2014.

Martin, J. A. (1985). Luke. In J. F. Walvoord & R. B. Zuck (Eds.), *The Bible Knowledge Commentary: An Exposition of the Scriptures* (Vol. 2). Wheaton, IL: Victor Books.